INTIMATE THOUGHTS OF GOD

What you are about to read, please remember

That God your Father in heaven, who loves you, and asks only that you obey his commandments and

Repent your sins, so when your time is up
He can say to you "Welcome"

OTHER BOOKS BY JAMES H. WHITE

I am The LORD thy GOD
In the Beginning —Bilingel
In the Beginning 2
There is NO Second Chance
Intimate thoughts of GOD

INTIMATE
THOUGHTS OF
GOD

JAMES WHITE

Order this book online at www.trafford.com
or email orders@trafford.com

Most Trafford titles are also available at major online book retailers.

Print information available on the last page.

ISBN: 978-1-4907-7567-8 (sc)
ISBN: 978-1-4907-7566-1 (e)

Scripture taken from The Holy Bible, King James Version. Cambridge Edition:
1769; King James Bible Online, 2016. www.kingjamesbibleonline.org.

Trafford rev. 10/21/2016

www.trafford.com

North America & international
toll-free: 1 888 232 4444 (USA & Canada)
fax: 812 355 4082

To the reader —This book is a labor of love-
"The cover says it all"!!! I have attempt to bring forth
Just what is Repent and why we should.

To sum it up all God ask of us is: To obey his Commandments and
Repent our sins before we pass on

"May this book be a blessing to you"

James White

CONTENTS

DEDICATION

This book is dedicated to our Lord and to
both of my Sons, James and David.

"Gone but never forgotten".

In the beginning was the Word, and the Word
was with God and the Word was God.

The same was in the beginning with God

All things were made by him, and without him
was not anything made that was made

In him was life; and the life was the light of men. (St. John 1-1).

Intimate Thoughts
of God Nov 2009

When something good or bad happens, what is the first thing you say—is it "Wow" or "No Way"—for the majority of us it is "Oh My God"! You have now—just at that moment—acknowledged that He is your God!

He is there for you when you call, but are you there for Him? God is always there for you in your time of need, whether it be joy or sorrow—Is it not GOD'S name the first thing you say? Why is this—would you say there is something unexplainable—for it seems that your first reaction is to call on your Father in Heaven, your God and Savior. Remember we were born in his image so why would He not love you.

Regardless of your faith we all have the Father, the Son, and the Holy Ghost, you pray to God, you ask Jesus Christ to forgive your sins, and you ask the Holy Ghost (Spirit) to come into your life.

Why is it that we only pay homage (respect) to God on Saturday, Wednesday and Sunday? Why don't you—as soon as your feet touch the floor each morning say, 'PRAISE GOD, PRAISE THE LORD, PRAISE BE YOUR HOLY NAMES,!

Now you are praising God every day, not just the established time as we know it. So if praise Him every morning—Why not praise and ask God to Bless your food at every meal. Your prayer need not be long—Just sincere and thankful. As an example: As a child looks at you with trusting eyes and says "I love you Daddy and Mummy", you feels tears come into your eyes. And you should feel the same way when you sincerely pray or think of God or His Son. What a wonderful example to show your children of your love for God.

ALWAYS, ALWAYS REMEMBER, GOD IS THERE FOR YOU!

1

'WHO IS GOD AND WHAT IS HE'

'"HE IS THE MOST MAGNIFICENT, WONDERFUL, LOVING FORGIVING GOD WHOM WE SHOULD HUMBLE OURSELF DAILY

GOD IS ALWAYS THERE AND IT MAKES NO DIFFERENCE WHETHER YOU ARE A JEW OR GENTILE =HE IS THERE FOR YOU—ALL HE ASK FOR HIS LOVE AND FORGIVENESS IS FOR YOU TO OBEY HIS COMMANDMENTS AND HIS SON—JESUS—COMMANDMENTS. ALSO

To repent your sins,

'TO KNOW GOD IS TO LOVE HIM AND YET FEAR HIM "FOR WE ALL ARE SINNERS BECAUSE WE DO NOT OBEY HIS COMMANDMENTS. DO YOU REMEMBER AS A CHILD THAT YOU DID SOMETHING THAT YOU WERE TOLD NOT TO DO, AND WHEN FACING YOUR PARENTS, FEARFUL OF THE CONSEQUENCE, FOR YOU KNEW YOU WERE WRONG

THERE IS NO DIFFERENCE WITH GOD'S COMMANDMENTS. WE FACE LIFE DAILY AND STRIVE TO DO WHAT OUR CONSCIOUS TELLS US AND HOPEFULLY IT IS RIGHT IN GOD'S EYES. THE FEAR THAT WE HAVE OF GOD, THAT WE CAN RECEIVE HIS LOVE AND FORGIVENESS IF WE ONLY WE "REPENT" OF OUR SINS THROUGH JESUS CHRIST HIS SON AND OUR SAVIOR,.

THIS WOULD BE THE MOST MAGNIFICENT GIFT YOU WILL EVER RECEIVE. THINK OF GOD AND IMAGE HIM IN YOUR MIND WITH HIS SON SITTING BESIDES

HIM—JUST WAITING FOR YOU TO SAY 'I REPENT OF ALL MY SINS, FORGIVE ME JESUS'

ALL THAT GOD AND JESUS ASK OF YOU IS TO OBEY THEIR COMMANDMENTS AND TO "SPREAD THE WORD OF THEIR LOVE AND FORGIVENESS. JESUS SAID 'ASK AND YOU SHALL RECEIVE', YOU MAY RECEIVE HIS GIFT IMMEDIATELY—AS IT HAPPEN TO ME—OR LATER ON, JUST BE PATIENT AND KEEP THE FAITH FOR THE LORD ALWAYS, KEEPS HIS WORD.'HUMBLE YOURSELF AND PRAY DAILY IF YOU WISH TO ENJOY THE GREATEST GIFT' HIS LOVE AND FORGIVENESS".

The Bible reveals God as the only Infinite and Eternal Being, having no beginning and no ending. He is the Creator and Sustainer of all things.

He is the Supreme Personal Intelligence, and Righteous of His universe.

He is life, and therefore, the only source of life. (John5:26)

Man is natural and cannot know God by wisdom. "Canst thou by searching find out God?" (Job 11:7) God is a person and can be known only by revelation. In the Old Testament He revealed Himself to and through His prophets. In the New Testament He reveals Himself through His

Son Jesus Christ. (Heb. 1:1-3)

THE EXISTENCE OF GOD

By faith Enoch was translated that he should not see death; and was not found, because God had translated him: for before his translation he had this testimony, that he pleased God But without faith it is impossible. To please Him: for he that cometh to God must believe that he is, and that He is a rewarder of them that diligently seek Him.

The Bible nowhere attempts to prove or argue the existence of God. "For he that cometh to God must believe He is". The existence of God is a fact taken for granted by the writers if both the Old and New Testaments. "In the beginning God"(Gen. 1;1). The Bible opens by announcing the sublime fact of God and His existence. There are arguments for the existence of God; they are not conclusive, but are food for thought.

(1) Universal belief in God comes from within man. It is innate in man, and comes formational intuition.

(2) The argument from "cause and effect" Everything that began owes its Existence to a cause. We have a watch, we must have watchmaker. We have a building; we must have a builder. We have a creation; we must have a creator. This creation could not have come into existence without an intelligent, personal creator any more than the alphabet could produce a book itself without the author

(3) The argument from anthropology. Man's moral and intellectual nature argues for moral and intellectual creator.

(4) The Bible and the Christ that it reveals, His virgin birth, His sinless life,

His vicarious death, and His bodily resurrection—all of this and much, much more—argue for the existence of God.

The Personality of God — (1 Thes. 1:9)

For they themselves show of us what manner of entering in we had unto you, and how ye turned to God from idols to serve the living and true God.

The Bible reveals God as a personality. He is called "the living and true God"—One possessing self-consciousness and self-determination. His Personality is shown in what He does, such as:

(1) God loves. "God so loved the world"(John 3:16)

(2) God hates. "These six things doth the Lord hate"(Prov. 6:16) (3) God cares. "He careth for you"(1 Peter 5:7)

(4) God grieves. "It grieved him at his heart(Gen. 6:6)

Only a personality can love, hate, care, and grieve, therefore, God must be a living, entemal, personal being.

THE NATURE OF GOD

He that loveth not knoweth not God; for God is love.

There are four definitions of God in the bible. Since God cannot be defined, they are incomplete. However, they do throw light upon the nature of God: They are:

(1) "God is love", This is the nature of God in His divine compassion.

(2) "God is light"(I John 1:5) This is the nature of God in His divine character; in Him there is no darkness.

(3) "God is consuming fire". (Heb. 12:29) This is the nature of God in His divined holiness.

(4) "God is a Spirit"(John 4:24) This is the nature of God in His divine essence.

The attributes of God reveal his nature. Do not think of His attributes

As abstract, but as vassal 'mediums through which His holy nature is unveiled.

—attributes ascribed to Him, such as:

(a) Life is ascribed to God (John5:26) (b) All knowledge is ascribed to God

© All power is ascribe to God(Rev. 9:6)

(d) Filling the universe with His presence is ascribed to God.

God is everywhere present, by the not in everything. If God were in everything, man could worship any object and he would be worshiping

God. God is a spirit being. "And they that worship him must worship him in spirit and truth."

THE GRACE OF GOD

For by grace are ye saved through faith; and that not of yourselves: it is the gift of God: Not of works, lest any man should boast.

Grace is the love and mercy of God in action. Mercy is negative, and Love is positive; both together mean grace. To show mercy in love is grace. God showed mercy in love when he sent his Son to bear our sins in His own body on the cross.(John 3:16)

(1) The grace of God saves forever. (Rom. 8:38, 39).

(2) The grace of God is unconditional, that is, we are not saved on the condition that we "hold out to the end" or that we "fail not" or that we" do our best". We are saved by the grace of God, apart from works.

(3) The grace of God is sufficient (IlCor. 12:9)

(4) The grace of God makes no discrimination (Rev. 22:17) (5) The grace of God justifies (Rom. 3:23, 24)

(6) The grace of God makes every believer an heir (Titus 3:7)

(7) The grace of God teaches the believer how to live Titus 2:11, 12)

The grace is nothing less than the unlimited love of God expressed in the gift of His Son, our Savior. It is the undeserved love of God towards sinners

By the Trinity of God we mean His tri-personal existence as Father, Son, and Holy Spirit—three distinct persons in one God.

WHY O'LORD WHY

I GLORIFY YOU, I PRAISE YOU

I LOVE YOU YET I CANNOT FIND YOU.
HELP ME LORD FOR I NEED YOU SO
CLEANSE MY HEART, OPEN MY EYES
AND TAKE THIS PAIN AWAY.
I PRAISE YOU AND I GLORIFY YOU LORD
LET ME FIND YOU BEFORE IT IS TO LATE.
PRAISE BE YOUR HOLY NAME.

GRANT ME PEACE O 'LORD

SINS AGAINST THE HOLY SPIRIT

Wherefore I say unto you, All manner of sin and blasphemy shall be forgiven unto men: but the blasphemy against the Holy Ghost shall not be forgiven unto men. And whosesoever speaketh a word against the Son of man, it shall be forgiven him: but whosoever speaketh against the Holy Ghost, it shall not be forgiven him, neither in this world, neither in the world to come.

This is a solemn study, because the Holy Spirit is God and can be sinned against by both the believer and the unbeliever. May He help you search your heart as consider:

(1) The sin of blaspheming the Holy Spirit (above verse) This sin is committed by unbelievers. It is often called the "unpardonable sin." It has no forgiveness. It was committed by the enemies of Jesus when they accused Him of casting out devils by the power of Satan (Matt. 12:24) when Jesus claimed to cast them out by the "Spirit of God."(Matt. 12:28).

(2) The sin of resisting the Holy Spirit (Acts 7:51) This sin is committed

By the unbeliever when rejecting Jesus Christ as Savior and Lord.

(3) The sin of grieving the Holy Spirit (Eph. 4:30-32). This sin is committed by believers. He is grieved by us unless He controls our lives to the glory of Jesus Christ.

(4) The sin of quenching the Holy Spirit (1 Thes. 5;19) This sin is committed by Christians when known sin is allowed to go unconfessed (1 John 1:9; also Isa. 59:1, 2).

(5) The sin of lying to the Holy Spirit (Acts 5; 1-11) The sin of Ananias and Sapphira was deception, born in jealousy. They tried to mock God (Gal. 6:7) The Holy Spirit can be sinned against, because He is God.

"BLESSED ARE THEY WHOSE TRANSGRESSIONS ARE FORGIVEN, WHOSE SINS ARE COVERED"

"BLESSED IS THE MAN WHOSE SINS THE LORD WILL NEVER COUNT AGAINST HIM".

"WHO IS IT THAT OVERCOMES THE WORLD-ONLY HE THAT BELIEVES THAT JESUS CHRIST IS THE SON OF GOD."

"I WILL PRAISE YOU, 0' LORD, WITH ALL MY HEART"
"I WILL TELL OF ALL YOUR WONDERS"
"I WILL BE GLAD AND REJOICE IN YOU."

"I WILL SING PRAISE TO YOUR HOLY NAME, 0' MOST HIGH"

JHW JUN 10

THE RESURRECTION
OF JESUS CHRIST

Jesus said "I am the resurrection and the life" (John 11:25), The Resurrection of Jesus Christ was the doctrine of every disciple, the faith of every true believer, the courage of every martyr, the theme of every sermon. And the power of ever evangelist.

Luke tells us that we have "many infallible proofs" of His resurrection (Acts 1:3) Let us look at some of these "infallible proofs" according to eye witnesses:

(1) After His resurrection He appeared first to Mary Magdalene (John 20:11-18).

(2) He appeared to the women returning from the sepulcher (Matt. 28:5-10). (3) Then he appeared to Peter (Luke 24:34)

(4) To the Emmaus disciples (Luke 24:13-31).

(5) To the apostles, Thomas not present (Luke 24:36-43). (6) Again to the apostles, Thomas present (John 20:24-29). (7) To the seven by the sea of Tiberius (John 21:1-23).

(8) To over five hundred brethren (1 Cor. 15:6). (9) He was seen of James (1 Cor. 15:7).

(10) He was seen again by the eleven apostles (Matt. 28:16-20) (Acts 1:3-12).

(11) He was seen of Stephen, the first martyr (Acts 7:55)

(12) He was seen of Paul on his way to Damascus (Acts 9:3-6)(1 Cor. 15:8) Many of these eye witnesses died martyrs' death because they preached

The resurrection of Jesus Christ. They were glad to die for a living Christ.

They had the "infallible proofs."

When Jesus was arrested in the Garden of Gethsemane, all of His disciples "forsook him and fled. (Matt. 26:56) From this time until after His resurrection, the disciples lived in fear. They did not believe that He would rise from the dead (John 20:9) Had Jesus not come from the dead, the cross would have been the end of Christianity. After the death of Jesus,

We see His disciples dejected, discouraged, and defeated. The death of Jesus meant but one thing to them: the end. How do we account for the great change that came into their lives three days and three nights later? The only logical explanation is that they had"

It is a Fact That Christ Died for You

For when we were without strength, in due time Christ dies for the ungodly.

For scarcely for a righteous man you will die: yet peradventure for a good man some would even dare to die.

But God commendeth his love towards us, in that, while we were yet sinners, Christ died for us.

He died for those who are unlike God. This includes you. "While we were yet sinners, Christ died for us (above verse)"

"For he (God the Father) hath made him (God the Son) to be made sin for us, who knew no sin; that we might be made the righteousness of God in him" (Page 326—11 Cor 5-21)

"For as much as ye know that ye were not redeemed with corruptible things, as silver and gold . . . But with the previous blood of Christ, as of a lamb without blemish and without spot" (Page 420—1 Peter 1'18, 19).

"For Christ also hath once suffered for sin, the just for the unjust, that he, should be bringing us to God, being put to death in this flesh but quickened in the spirit" (Page 423—1 Peter 3:18,)

"Christ died for our sins according to the Scriptures (Page 317—1 Cor. 15:3).

In the light of these wonderful Scriptures, will you now thank God for His great love in sending His Son to bear your sins in His own body on the cross, and admit to yourself that: Christ died on Calvary for me."

Jesus and the Two Births

There was a man of the Pharisees, named Nic-o-de'-mus, a ruler of the Jews. The same came to Jesus by night, and said unto him, Rabbi, we know that thou art a teacher come from God: for no man can do these miracles that thou doest, except God be with him.

Jesus answered and said unto him, Verily, verily, I say unto thee, Except a man be born again, he cannot see the kingdom of God "Nic-o-de'-mus said unto him, How can a man be born when he is old"? Can he enter the second time into his mother's womb, and be born? Jesus answered, Verily, verily, I say unto thee. Except a man be born of water and of the Holy Spirit, he cannot enter into the kingdom of God.

That which is born of the flesh is flesh; and that which is born of the Spirit is Spirit. Marvel not that I said unto thee, "Ye must be born again.: The wind bloweth where it listeth, and thou hearest the sound thereof, but canst not tell whence it cometh, and whither it goes: so is every one that is born of the Spirit.

In the Scriptures, we see "'Jesus and Nicodemus face to face—Jesus the Son of God, and Nicodemus the son of natural man.'"

Nicodemus was a very religious man, but he was not a child of God What a shock it must have been. To learn his that his religion was not enough! It never 1s.

He came to Jesus, addressing Him as "a teacher come from God. Jesus knew Nicodemus," as He knows all men and Jesus knew he needed more than a teacher—he needed a Savior, He needed more than religion—he needed regeneration. He needed more than law—he needed life

Jesus began by going right to the point when he said "Ye must be born again." Nicodemus asked, "How can man be born when he is old?" Then Jesus pointed out the dissimilarity in the two births, "'That which is born of flesh is flesh" (the flesh will never change): and that which is born of the Spirit is Spirit" Other spirit will never change,.

First, let's take a brief at the flesh birth.

(1) It produces an old, sinful nature (Ps. 51:5 OT).

(2) It produces a corruptible nature (Page 420—1 Peter 1:23)

(3) It produces an old nature under the sentence of death (Page 281—Rom. 6:23)

(4) It produces an old nature that makes every unsaved person a child of the devil (Page 435—1 John 3:10, also Page 181-John 8:44).

Second, let us say a word about the new birth:

(1) It produces a sinless nature (Page 435—1 John3:9)

(2) It produces a nature that cannot sin (Page 435-1 John 3:9) (3) it produces a righteous nature (Page 326—11 Cor. S:21)

(4) It produces a divine nature (Page 426—11 Peter 1:4)

Every born-again person has two natures: the old from the old birth, and the new from the new birth. By the old birth, we are children of the flesh; by the new birth, we are children of God. This is why "Ye must be born again."

ISAIAH

(New Testament page 247)

0 Lord; in these things is the life of my spirit Oh, restore me to health Lo!, it was for my welfare that I had great bitterness; but thou has held back my life from the Pit, thou has cast my sins behind thy back. For the dead cannot thank thee; those who go down to the Pit cannot hope for thy faithfulness.

The living, the living, he thanks thee, as I do this day; the father makes known to the children thy faithfulness. And we will sing to stringed instruments all the days of our life, at the house of the Lord.

DOES GOD ANSWER
ALL PRAYERS?

If ye abide in me, and my words abide in you, ye shall ask what you will, and it shall be done unto you.

The Bible is filled with answered prayers from Genesis to Revelation. You are commanded to pray, and God has promised to answer (Jer. 33:3 OT) In the above Scripture, there are two requirements for answers to prayer. First, you are to abide in Him; that is, to continue in Him. It means to remain in His perfect will at all cost (Page 291—Rom. 12:1, 2), Second, His words are to abide in you; they are to become a vital part of your life. You are to be filled with, and guided by, His words (Page 364—Col. 3:16, 17). Meet these two requirements, and your prayers will be answered.

(1) The answered is sometimes immediate. Peter walked on the water to go to Jesus, and as he begins to sink, he prayed, "Lord, save me." The answer was immediate (Page 29 — Matt. 14:22-31)

(2) The answer is sometimes delayed. The delay is according to His will (Page 284—Rom. 8:28). The resurrection of Lazarus is a good example of delayed answer to prayer. Lazarus was sick. Mary and Martha sent for Jesus to come and heal him. But Jesus delayed coming until Lazarus was dead and in the tomb for four days. Then He came and raised Lazarus from the dead. The answer was delayed—but not denied (Page 185— John 11:1-44)

(3) The answer is sometimes "no". When God answers with a "no", He always accompanies the answer with peace (Page 358—Phil. 4:6, 7) and grace (Page 333—11 Cor. 12:7-10)

(4) The answer is sometimes different from what you expect. You for patience and God sends tribulation— because "tribulation worketh patience" (Page278—Rom. 5:3) God answers all your prayers—not according to your wishes, but according to His perfect will.

WHAT IS FAITH?

Now faith is the substance of things hoped for, the evidence of things not seen. For by it the elders obtain a good report. Through faith we understand that the worlds were framed by the word of God, so that things which are seen were not made of things which do appear.

(1) Faith is the substance (title deed) of things hoped for . . . ." Your faith is your title deed to eternal life. Just as a title deed is evidence of real estate, so your faith is evidence of your eternal estate in God (Page 324—11 Cor. 4:18) (1) Faith is taking God at His word. And asking no questions (Page 407 Heb. 11:6).

(2) Faith is knowing that:" All things work together for good to them that love God" (Page 284—Rom. 8:28) Faith does not believe that all things are good, or that all things work well, It does believe that all things (good or bad) work together for good to them that love God.

(3) Faith has two sides. One side has to do with the intellect. It is an intellectual conviction that Jesus Christ is God. The other side has to do with the will. It is a volitional surrender of the will to Jesus Christ as Master.

This is seen when Thomas believed and confessed, "My Lord and my God"(Page 206—John 20:28). "My Lord"—that was volition surrender. "My God"—this was intellectual conviction. Together you have saving faith (Page 206—John 20:31).

Saving faith is an intellectual conviction that Jesus is God, and a volitional surrender to Him as Lord (Master) of your life. By faith, the mind trusts in God:—the heart responds to the love of God; the will submits to the command of God; and the life obeys in the service of God.

(4) Faith is paradoxical. It goes beyond reason. It believes without understanding "why". It sings in prison (Page 244—Acts 16:25). It glories in tribulations (Page 278 —Rom. 5:3). It chooses to suffer (Page 408—Heb. 11:25). it accepts all things as a part of God's will (Page 353—Phil. 1:12).

You are born with this faith. It comes by hearing the Word of God (Page 288—Rom. 10:17), This is why we are commanded to preach the gospel to every creature, that they may hear and believe (Page 287—Rom. l0:13, 14).

THE IMPORTANCE OF FAITH

Above all, taking the shield of faith, wherewith ye shall be able to quench all the fiery darts of the wicked.

The shield of faith is a vital part of the Christian's armor. You are to put on the "whole armor of God"(above verses 10-18), because the Christian life is a warfare, a spiritual conflict. As Paul names the different parts of the Christian's armor, he comes to the shield and emphasizes its importance by saying, "Above all, taking the shield of faith . . . "for with the shield of faith, nothing can hurt you"; you are more than conquerors through Him (Page 285—Rom. 8:37)

The importance of faith is seen in that:—

(1) You cannot be saved without faith (Page 168—John 3:36).

(2) You cannot live victoriously over the world without faith (Page 439—1 John 5:4), (3)

To Those Who Have Lost A Love One

He is gone, not for awhile
Not for weeks
He is gone for eternity.
How I long for his look,
His slowly grin as his eyes
Speak his' love
Why, 0 GOD, Why
We had just found each other.

Anticipating or Dreams

Oh my children

How my heart aches,
For the dreams I held
You have taken away,
As man turned to dust
So have my dreams of you.

"A Daily Prayer"

OUR FATHER WHICH IS IN HEAVEN

HALLOWED BE THY NAME: THY KINGDOM COME. THY WILL BE ONE IN EARTH, AS IT IS IN HEAVEN. GIVE US THIS DAY OUR DAILY BREAD. AND FORGIVE US OUR DEBTS AS WE FORGIVE OUR DEBTORS AND LEAD US NOT INTO TEMPTATION,

BUT DELIVER US FROM EVIL: FOR THINE IS THE KINGDOM, AND THE POWER. AND THE GLORY, FOREVER AMEN

WHEN YOU GO TO BED"

AS I LAY ME DOWN TO SLEEP.
IF I SHOULD DIE BEFORE I WAKE
I PRAY 1liE LORD MY SOUL TO KEEP AMEN.

"WHEN YOU EAT"

GOD IS GOOD.
GOD IS GREAT,
I THANK. YOU FOR THIS FOOD AMEN

Thank You Father

I thank you Father for all you have given us

You gave us the Earth with the stars above

You gave us the air to breath and water to drink

You gave us the ocean with fish to eat

All the animals you provided for us

You made man from dust and women from man

You have given us everything

All You ask is that we obey your Commandments.

But man has been evil and sinful from the beginning

You tried and tried with Moses, Elijah, Jacob and others

Yet no one would listen and so He said enough is enough

I will destroy earth and all living things on it.

But God repented and ask Noah to build an Ark.

Within that Ark Noah was to put two of all the living animals, male and female,

With his family only as all others thought him mad to build an Ark in the desert.

The rains came for forty days and night and covered the earth and no living

Creature survived, only Noah, his family and the animals.

After the rain stopped Noah sent birds out to see if they could find land

Time went by and one day a bird brought a twig with a green leaf which indicated that the waters were receding.

Land appeared and Noah released all the animals

This was the beginning of the New Testament and of our

Lord Jesus being born

On the morning of 30 October 1995 at 520 am I had the urge to write the following:

Here I am O 'Lord with all my suffering and troubles

Here I am O 'Lord, I love you and trust you, use me O 'Lord

For I am lost without you.

Our Father sent you to guide us and to forgive us our sins. Help us O'Lord

For I have sinned

Forgive me Lord and guide me

Here I am O 'Lord

Here I am

This was written during Church services sometime during the summer of 2002

Why O 'Lord why

I glorify you, I praise you, I love you yet I cannot find you.

Help me Lord for I need you so

Cleanse my heart, open my eyes and take this pain away.

I Glorify and Praise you Lord

Please give me peace and take this pain away

Let me find you Lord

Before it is too late

James H. White

15 Nov 2003

"For The Lost Ones"

WHY O' LORD WHY?
I GLORIFY YOU, I PRAISE YOU
I LOVE YOU, YET I CANNOT FIND YOU
HELP ME LORD FOR I NEED YOU
SO CLEANSE MY HEART
OPEN MY EYES
TAKE THIS PAIN AWAY
I LOVE YOU SO LORD
I PRAISE YOUR HOLY NAME
LET ME FIND YOU LORD
BEFORE IT IS TOO LATE
TAKE THIS PAIN AWAY
GIVE ME PEACE

"PRAISE HIM"

TO YOU LORD GOD I GIVE MY BODY AND SOUL
I PRAY TO YOU AND I KNOW YOU ARE LISTING
I PRAISE YOU MORNING NOON AND NIGHT
I THANK YOU FOR YOUR SON JESUS CHRIST
WHO IS MY SAVIOR, I LOVE YOU BOTH
GUIDE ME FATHER
HELP ME TO GLORIFY YOUR NAME
HOW GREAT AND COMPASSION YOU ARE
ALL YOU ASK OF US IS TO OBEY YOUR COMMANDMENTS

"BLESSED IS THE NATION WHOSE GOD
IS LORD" PSALM 33:12 (NIV)

James White

THE RIGHTEOUS WILL LIVE BY FAITH FROM GOD AND IN JESUS CHRIST TO ALL WHO BELIEVE.

This is an another verse along the same theme

Lookup
Look down
Look all around and see all the miracles abound
The sky, the sun, the moon and stars
Feel the air around you
Taste the rain as it falls
For all is given to you by the one above
You're heavenly Father, our Lord
Known to all as our God. With all the miracles we see
His greatest miracle of all was the birth of his son Jesus Christ
Whom we proclaim as our Savior.
Praise God—-lift up your voice and give thanks for all the miracles abound
Praise him our most heavenly Father for his Son, our Savior Jesus Christ Praise
him morning and night
Praise him, Praise him.
Praise him

These come to me on three separated occasions during the time Mike Taylor was the music director (1998)? I thought these wools would make a great song;

Look up look down
Look all around
See the miiacles around you
Believe in Him
Believe in Him for he is your Father
Believe in him—all he asks you is for you to obey his Commands

He is all forgiving Believe in Him Believe in Him

Lookup
Look down
Look all around
The Father is everywhere
He has given you life
All he asks is to
Obey his Commandments
Obey his Commandments
For he is your Father
He giveth and taketh away
To save my soul Father I will obey
I love you Father and I praise you.
Lookup
Look down
Look all around and see the miracles
For he is everywhere

James H. White
16 November 2003

HERE I AM O'LORD

WITH ALL MY SUFFERING AND TROUBLES
HERE I AM O'LORD
I TRUST YOU
I LOVE YOU
HELP ME LORD FOR I AM LOST WITHOUT YOU
OUR FATHER SENT YOU TO LOVE AND GUIDE US
AND TO FORGIVE OUR SINS
HELP US O 'LORD FOR WE HAVE SINNED
FORGIVE US O 'LORD, GUIDE US IN YOUR WAY
HERE I AM O 'LORD
HERE I AM.

MIRACLES

LOOK UP, LOOK DOWN
LOOK AROUND-
SEE THE MIRACLES ABOUND. THE SKY. THE CLOUDS.
THE MOON, THE STARS AND THE SUN.
THE AIR WE BREATH, THE WATER WE DRINK
ALL OF THESE MIRACLES WE TAKE FOR GRANTED-
WAS AND STILL IS GIVEN TO US BY THE LORD OUR GOD,
AND ALL HE ASK IN RETURN IS TO OBEY HIS
COMMANDMENTS
HE GAVE US HIS GREATEST MIRACLE, HIS SON JESUS
CHRIST
WHO BECAME OUR SAVIOUR.
THIS MIRACLE ALONE SHOWS HIS LOVE FOR ALL OF US.
WE THANK YOU LORD WITH ALL OUR HEART
FOR ALL OF YOUR MIRACLES-PRAISE BE YOUR HOLY
NAME.

Isaiah

(New Testament page 247)

When God ask, what have you done that has pleases me/Have you keep my commandments/Have you taught your children and grandchildren hat I am the "Creator" What will be your answer/If it is "yes my Lord"-then He will bless you and say "Welcome", but if it is "no my Lord" guess where your next place will be.

A Profound Statement

"All your life has been a preparation for dying"!
Preparation to me means that we should be living by GOD'S
And LORD Jesus Christ Commandments every day. Now if we find
We slide a little, we are internal grateful that God's son Jesus
Was given to mankind for repentance of his sins

(Author unknown)

About the Author
and his Blessings

The sky was so beautiful with its background of pale blues and white clouds. It was so quiet that it seemed as if time had stood still. It just did not seem possible that only a few miles away in the jungle, the war was still raging on. As I sat on the rooftop reading a western paperback, I heard a voice that seemed to say my name. I saw no one and continued to read. Again, I heard a voice, this time I looked all around and saw no one and then I looked at the sky and saw our Savior, Jesus Christ, all in white with the gold sash around his middle and he was standing in the sky with his arms outstretched, you could see the nail holes in his hands.

As I looked upon his face I saw tears flowing down his cheeks. I looked away for I could not believe what I saw, but as I looked again Jesus Christ was still there. The tears were there as if he was taking all the suffering going on in Vietnam upon himself. Needless to say, I fell to my knees with tears flowing from my eyes. After a few moments I opened my eyes again and Jesus was gone.

As God is my Heavenly Father, I was blessed to see his Son. I asked others if they saw, but no one had. I was doing nothing related to religion, so my question has always been. Why me Lord?" Maybe this book is the reason.

My second Blessing occurred on December 14, 1988, at my church. I had just learned that my son David had died. The pain was so intense; it was if I had a nail in my heart. I went into the sanctuary and sat down. My grief was so great I could hardly breathe. My tears would not stop. My Pastor came to me and asked what was wrong. I told him and he said, "let us pray." We did and afterwards I said I would like to be alone. After he left, I arose and knelt at the altar and cried out to

God saying, "You lost your Son and you know the pain, now I have lost mine, please take this pain from me." At that very instant the pain was gone and a peace came upon me. To this day I think of my son only with tears, but no pain.

My third Blessing was more recent. My knees had been injured when I was in the Army paratroopers and I had to use crutches when the pain became unbearable. The doctors said I must have both knees replaced but I said later. Again I went to God and asked for his help and praying to him to take this pain away and immediately I got up and walked without crutches. Additional help also came from a stranger who asked if I had tried a herb compound called Glucosamine/Chondroitin/MSM. I said no, but I'll try anything. He emphasized it must contain MSM. I take 3 tablets a day and with faith in God, I put the crutches away.

Some would say that I am witnessing and they would be right. I want everyone in the world to know God is always there for you. You may receive an answer to your request immediately or it may come about in another way. The main thing is always have faith, read your Bible and praise God.

The author is a retired officer who served in the United States Marine Corps and the United States Army and was medically discharged on May 1, 1972. Jim and his wife, Brenda, now reside in Broad Creek, North Carolina, where they can look upon God's beautiful array of wondrous works displayed in his bountiful waters and glorious sunsets. God's works are all around us. Just look, listen and hear—His Miracles—they are all around you.

Printed in the United States
By Bookmasters